Omnibus Press

London/New York/Sydney/Cologne

© Copyright 1987 Omnibus Press/Bobcat Books
(A Division of Book Sales Limited)

ISBN 0.7119.1376.5
Order No. OP 44528

Exclusive distributors:
BOOK SALES LIMITED
8/9 Frith Street, London W1V 5TZ, UK.
MUSIC SALES CORPORATION
24 East 22nd Street, New York, NY 10010, USA.
MUSIC SALES LIMITED
GPO Box 3304, Sydney, NSW 2001, Australia.
To the Music Trade only:
MUSIC SALES LIMITED
8/9 Frith Street, London W1V 5TZ, UK.

Text and Design by Susan Black.
Picture credits: Bob Ramirez, Dan Jones, Robin Ross, Don Powers,
Larry Busacca, Retna Pictures, Photo Alvarez.

Typeset by Capital Setters Limited.
Printed in England by J.B. Offset Printers (Marks Tey) Limited, Marks Tey.

Madonna is the most successful female pop singer of all time – and that's official.

Her 1987 'Who's That Girl' tour places her firmly amongst the megastars of the eighties in terms of ticket sales while her unbroken string of over a dozen hit singles gives her a massive statistical edge over any other contenders.

By the end of the tour Madonna had performed before nearly two million fans in three continents. In London alone the elaborately staged show was seen by over 200,000 people who packed into Wembley stadium for three separate concerts. Outside Wembley ticket touts were asking – and receiving – £30 to £35 each for £15 tickets.

In the history of rock and pop, only David Bowie has attempted to produce a show of such striking stagemanship. Madonna's ninety-minute plus extravaganza featured complex dance routines, an ever-changing stage set, back projection, umpteen costume changes and simultaneous video projection to ensure that those at the back had a reasonable chance of seeing Madonna clearly.

This was essential – for Madonna does not so much *sing* a song as *perform* her repertoire, either replicating her videos or acting out a song's lyric with gestures and movement. Between songs she deals as confidently with massive, and occasionally abusive, crowds as any rock performer before her. At Wembley, clearly distressed when cans were thrown on stage, Madonna threatened not to cast her spare knickers into the crowd unless the can throwing ceased. It did.

Show followed show in precise detail; each musician and dancer was cued in to every move. There was no room for spontaneity in a production of this kind. For the opening number, 'Open Your Heart', Madonna appeared atop a flight of glittered steps dressed in her black figure hugging corset, a foundation garment upon which all the evening's costume changes would be layered. It was clear that this Madonna had shed stones in weight since the Madonna of the 'Like A Virgin' tour. Madonna 1987 was sleek and svelte, fit as an Olympic athlete, a ball of energy honed to perfection through strict dieting and a daily regimen of exercise that demanded considerable discipline.

Hit followed hit like a jukebox stuffed with coins. 'True Blue' followed 'Lucky Star' and Madonna wore a blue fifties-style dress à la video; 'La Isla Bonita' followed 'Papa Don't Preach' and Madonna wore a red Spanish flamenco skirt; 'Material Girl' followed 'Dress You Up' and Madonna wore horn-rimmed glasses, a red hat and a top draped with bijouterie of all shapes and sizes. The show climaxed with a series of planned encores including 'Into The Groove' and 'Holiday', both hip-numbers that cued the audience into frenetic dancing.

Overall, Madonna impresses as a *performer* rather than a singer, a dancer of flair and untiring energy, a star in the Hollywood (rather than the rock) tradition.

Long may she reign.

Madonna: Quotes

"I have my moments of exhaustion . . . but I can go for nights without sleeping if I'm not working on anything specifically. But if I'm doing a tour or working on a film I really have to be on the ball so I make sure I get to bed early. I need at least six hours sleep so I have to cut down on my social life if I want to feel good the next day. When I occasionally get eight hours sleep I find it hard to believe."

"I went to a Catholic school and my father was very strict and a disciplinarian – we had to go to church every morning before we went to school. When we got home we'd get changed, do our chores, do our homework and eat supper. I wasn't even allowed to watch television until late in my teens. My father didn't like us having idle time on our hands. If we didn't have homework he'd find us something to do around the house – he was very adamant about us being productive. My father came from a very poor family, his parents were Italian immigrants. He was the youngest of six boys and was the only one who got a college education so it was very important to him that we made the best of our educational opportunities. I turned down a scholarship to the University of Michigan and when I told him I didn't want to go to college but wanted to go to New York and be a dancer it didn't make any sense to him. To him dancing was a hobby and not something you could make a living from."

"My ballet teacher is a real adventurous spirit and would be pleased with anything I did but I can't say that my father had the same reaction. I never dressed that way around the house but I left home at 17 and didn't go home that often. It's taken a few years to get closer to my family again. There was a time when we weren't talking a lot. It wasn't a case of me just having to go away and make my own way in life. I just didn't feel that he'd truly understand or appreciate it until later."

"Madonna is my mother's name and she died when I was very young and I loved her a lot so that alone means a lot to me. She was sweet, beautiful and a hard worker. Sometimes I think about how like her I might be but I'll never know – I tend to romanticise and fantasise about it all the same. It's very rare for an Italian Catholic mother to name her daughter after her – especially as it's such a rare name – so I think maybe it was meant to happen that she died when I was so young. But somehow her spirit is inside of me. But I've inherited some of my father's qualities – stubbornness and being a killjoy. If I go out with friends I'm usually the first one who wants to go home in spite of their protests. When we went to visit relatives my father would always want to go home instead of spending the night with them. That's my father in me."

"I want to be a symbol of something. That's what I think when I think of conquering. It's that you stand for something. I mean, as far as I'm concerned, Marilyn Monroe conquered the world. She stands for something."

"I like to have control over most of the things in my career but I'm not a tyrant. I don't have to have it on my album that it's written, arranged, produced, directed and stars Madonna. To me, to have total control means you can lose objectivity. What I like is to be surrounded by really talented, intelligent people you can trust. And ask them for their advice and get their input. But let's face it, I'm not going to make an album and not show up for the vocals or make a video and have nothing to do with the script."

"I think women are intimidated by women who are incredibly ambitious or competitive because it's easier to deal with girls who aren't. It's easier to deal with people who aren't. But I never really think consciously of the fact that I'm a girl or anything like that. In fact, I think I've had advantages because I'm a girl."

"I think I have an original sense of style, and I think that people are unconsciously copying my style. My style is a combination of a lot of things and maybe theirs is too. Either it's coincidence or they're copying my style – it's just obvious. But sometimes, when you see people do that, it's really cute, you know? But sometimes it isn't."

"I see (my own image on the screen above the stage) and I say, 'Oh God. What have I done? What have I created? Is that me, or is this me, this small person standing here on the stage?' That's why I call the tour Who's That Girl: because I play a lot of characters, and every time I do a video or a song, people go, 'Oh, *that's* what she's like.' And I'm not like any of them. I'm all of them. I'm none of them. You know what I mean?"

"I've changed my image. If you spend a couple of years wearing lots of layers of clothes and tons of jewellery, it takes you forever to get dressed. And if your hair is long and crazy, you just get the urge to take it all off, strip yourself down and cut your hair just for relief. Everybody does that, you know."

"I liked my body when I was growing up and I wasn't ashamed of it. I liked boys and didn't feel inhibited around them. Maybe it comes from having brothers and sharing a bathroom. The boys got the wrong impression of me at high school. They mistake forwardness for promiscuity. When they don't get what they want they turn on you. I went through a period when all the girls thought I was loose and the boys said I was a nymphomaniac. The first boy I ever slept with was my boyfriend and we'd been going out a long time."

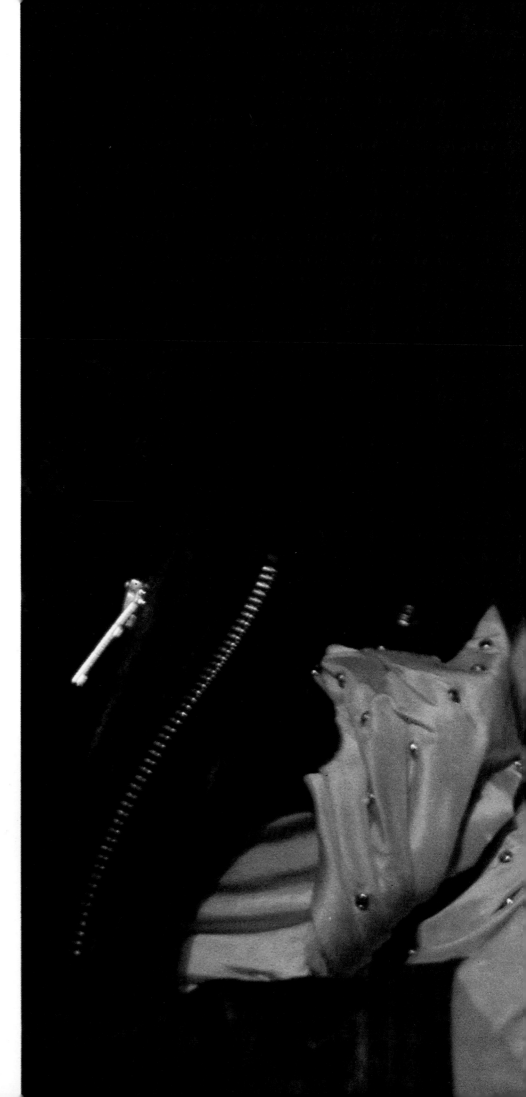

"It really annoyed me that most of the dancers I knew had such a simple minded view of life. They were really closed up. They got up early, took dance classes all day, and then they went to rehearsal and ate healthy food. Then they went home and went to bed early. They did this every day and they didn't know anything about music or art; they just knew nothing and were completely ignorant. And most of the kids that I knew who were in my ballet class and stuff, were little bratty girls who stared at themselves in the mirror all day. I found myself doing the same thing, ultimately, that I did when I was living in Detroit. I started rebelling and wanting to get out. All these girls would come to class with black leotards and pink tights and their hair up in buns with little flowers in it. So I cut my hair really short and I'd grease it so it would be sticking up, and I'd rip my tights so there were runs all over them and I'd make a big cut down the middle of my leotard and put safety pins all the way up it. Anything to stand out from them and say, 'I'm not like you, OK. I'm taking dance classes and everything but I'm not stuck here like you.' Eventually I said to myself, 'Well, if you don't like it Madonna, do what you want to do, you know you can dance. You've made a lot of friends, you know musicians, so go do what you want to do.' That's when I started exploring other territories and quit going to dance class every day."

"When I was in tenth grade I knew a girl who was a serious ballet dancer. She looked smarter than your average girl in an interesting off-beat way so I attached myself to her and she took me to ballet classes. I met Christopher Flynn, a tutor who saved me from my high school turmoil. I loved him. He was a mentor and a father, an imaginary lover . . . he encouraged me to go to New York. He was the one who told me I could do it if I wanted to."

"I've been upset but I would always go onstage. I like to try to fix it first, though. I've had fights with people right before I've gone onstage, and then I've gone onstage with tears in my eyes. I would always go onstage unless something truly horrible happened."

"I swore after my last tour that I wasn't going to do another. That whole living out of a suitcase business – I don't know how Bruce Springsteen does it. I could never go on tour for a year. I told my manager that the only way I would do the tour is if I could make it interesting for myself. Because that was the challenge: being able to make a show interesting in a stadium, where you're not *supposed* to be interesting, where it's just this big mega-show, real impersonal. I wanted to make it really personal, even though people would be sitting really far away from me. And I think that's what we've managed to do."

"I think I stand for a whole lot of things in fans' minds, a lot of kinds of stereotypes, like the whole sex-goddess image and the blonde thing. But mainly I think that they feel that most of my music is really, really positive, and I think they appreciate that, particularly the women. I think I stand for everything they're really taught *not* to be, so maybe I provide them with a little bit of encouragement."

"Music is a very personal statement, but I've always liked to have different characters that I project. I feel that I projected a very specific character for 'Like A Virgin' and that whole business and then created a much different character for my third album. The problem is, in the public's mind, you are your image, your musical image, and I think that those characters are only extensions of me. There's a little bit of you in every character that you do. I think I had something in common with Susan in *Desperately Seeking Susan* and I think I have a lot in common with Nikki Finn in *Who's That Girl*, but it's not me. Still . . . I wouldn't have been attracted to her if we didn't have something in common."

"I was surprised with how people reacted with 'Like A Virgin' because when I did the song, to me, I was singing about how something made me feel a certain way – brand-new and fresh – and everyone else interpreted it as 'I don't want to be a virgin any more. Fuck my brains out!' That's not what I sang at all."

"People have this idea that if you're sexual and beautiful and provocative, then there's nothing else you could possibly offer. People have always had that image about women. And while it might have seemed like I was behaving in a stereotypical way, at the same time I was also masterminding it. I was in control of everything I was doing, and I think that when people realised that, it confused them. It's not like I was saying, 'Don't pay any attention to the clothes – to the lingerie – I'm wearing.' Actually, the fact that I was wearing those clothes was meant to drive home the point that you can be sexy and strong at the same time. In a way it was necessary to wear the clothes."

"I don't think about the work I do in terms of feminism. I certainly feel that I give women strength and hope, particularly young women. So in that respect, I feel my behaviour is feminist. But I'm certainly not militant about it, nor do I exactly premeditate it."

"I think people have too many pretentious ideas about what's artistic and what has integrity and what doesn't. They think if it's simple and accessible, then it's commercial and a total compromise. And if it's masked in mystery, not completely understood and slightly unattractive, it has integrity and is artistic. I don't believe that."

"When women didn't like me I simply chalked it up to the reason women *always* have a problem with me: I think that women who are strong, or women who wanted to be strong or be respected, were taught that they had to behave like men, or *not* be sexy or feminine or something, and I think it pissed them off that I was doing that. Also, I think for the most part men have always been the aggressors sexually. Through time immemorial they've always been in control. So I think sex is equated with power in a way, and that's scary. It's scary for men that women should have that power, and I think it's scary for women to have that power – or to have that power and be sexy at the same time."

"Why aren't (critics) letting (sexuality) stand in the way of appreciating Prince's music? He was certainly just as sexually provocative, if not more than I was. I wasn't talking about giving *head*. He was much more specific than I was."

"Plenty of people are getting my message. I'm not going to change the world in a day. I don't know . . . maybe it never will be where men and women are equal. They're too different. I mean . . . it just seems that as long as women are the ones that give birth to children, it'll never really change. I'm not saying that in a sad way. I think more and more women will be able to have more freedom to do whatever they want, and they won't have so many prejudices thrown at them, but I think it would be much too idealistic to say that one day we will never be discriminated against because we're women."

"At first I enjoyed the comparisons between me and (Marilyn Monroe). I saw it as a compliment: she was very sexy – *extremely* sexy – and she had blonde hair, and so on and so forth. Then it started to annoy me because nobody wants to be continuously reminded of someone else. You want people to see that you have a statement of your own to make."

"When (the nude pictures) were taken eight years ago they weren't meant for publication in any magazine. They were taken by these guys who took pictures for nude exhibitions. At the time I wasn't well known and wasn't aware that I was setting myself up for a future scandal. For years I modelled for lots of life studies in art schools. I was a dancer at the time. I was in really good shape and slightly underweight so you could see my muscle definition and my skeleton. I was one of their favourite models because I was easy to draw. I did that work to make money and ended up modelling privately in people's houses so I got involved with photographers. I consider the nude a work of art. I don't see pornography in Michaelangelo. Obviously I would have preferred they weren't published but I think when people saw them they said, 'What's the big deal?' It's other people's problems if they turn them into something smutty. That was never my intention."

"At first the *Playboy* photos were very hurtful to me, and I wasn't sure how I felt about them. Now I look back at them and I feel silly that I ever got upset, but I *did* want to keep some things private. It was like when you're a little girl at school and some nun comes and lifts up your dress in front of everybody and you get really embarrassed. It's not really a terrible thing in the end, but you're not ready for it, and it seems so awful and you seem so exposed. Also, *Penthouse* did something really nasty: they sent copies of the magazine to Sean. That whole time was almost too much. I didn't think I was going to be married with 13 helicopters flying over my head. It turned into a circus. In the end I was laughing. At first I was outraged and then I was laughing. You couldn't have written it in a movie. No one would have believed it. It was better than anything like that . . . it was just incredible. It was like a Busby Berkeley musical. Or something that someone would stage to generate a lot of publicity for one of their stars."

"From the time we got married (I get the feeling that people want our marriage to fail) they couldn't make up their minds: they wanted me to be pregnant, or they wanted us to get a divorce. That put a lot of strain on our relationship, too, after a while. It's been a character building experience, and a test of love to get through it all."

"A lot of times the press would make up the most awful things that we had never done, fights that we never had. Then sometimes we *would* have a fight, and we'd read about it, and it would be almost spooky, like they'd predicted it or they'd bugged our phones or they were listening in our bedroom. It can be very scary if you let it get to you."

"Sean will always deal with the press in his own way. For myself I *have* accommodated the press a great deal. I've done numerous press conferences, numerous press interviews. But I'm a lot more outgoing and verbal in that way than Sean is. Also, in the beginning of my career, I invited controversy and press and publicity, and I don't think that he did at all. He was a very serious actor, and he wasn't interested in having a Hollywood star image and didn't do a lot of interviews, and it took him quite by surprise, whereas I had already kind of thrown myself into that world. And therefore we deal with it differently."

"I don't like violence. I never condoned hitting anyone, and I never thought that any violence should have taken place. But on the other hand I understand Sean's anger, and believe me I've wanted to hit (the press) many times. I never *would*, you know, because I realise that it would just make things worse. Besides, I have chances to vent my anger in ways other than confrontation. I like to fight people and kind of manipulate them into feeling like they're not being fought. I'd rather do it that way."

"I think (Sean) really believes it's a waste of energy. It antagonises the press and generates even more publicity and I think he realises that. But once (the press) realised he was a target for that, they really went out of their way to pick on him, to the point where they would walk down the street and say, 'C'mon, c'mon, hit me, hit me.' It's not fair. And they insult me, and they try to get him to react. You just have to have the strength to rise above it all."

"There have been times when I've thought, 'If I'd known it was going to be like this, I wouldn't have tried so hard.' But I feel that what I do affects people in a very positive way. That's the most important thing, and that's what I always set out to do. And you can't affect people in a large grand way without being scrutinised and judged and put under a microscope, and I accept that. If it ever gets too much, or I feel like I'm being over scrutinised, or I'm not enjoying it any more, then I won't do it."

"We are a 'Hollywood couple' so people are going to pay a lot of attention to our marriage and whether it's going to work or not. If we have our fights . . . I think that's pretty normal for young people in the first few years of marriage. It's normal for anybody who's married, but when you put all the pressure that we've had on top of that, I think the fact that we're still together is pretty amazing. You know, we're working it out . . . it's easy to give up but not easy for me to give up."

"I don't go to church but I believe in God. When I was little I had all the usual feelings of guilt. I was very conscious of God watching everything I did. Until I was 12 I believed the devil was in the basement and I would run up the stairs fast so he wouldn't grab my ankles. I've always carried around a few rosaries. There was a turquoise coloured one my grandmother gave me a long time ago which I wore as a necklace. It isn't sacrilegious to me. I thought the huge crucifixes nuns wore with their habits were beautiful."

"I guess a lot of my hot-blooded and passionate temperament is Italian. I like dark brooding men with rough tempers. Italian men like to dominate and sometimes I like to cast myself in the submissive role."

"I didn't have a very happy time in England during filming for SHANGHAI EXPRESS at Elstree. The press here were unbelievably vicious and rude. I like England but it isn't what I'm used to. In New York people are loud and say what they want. English people are far more reserved. If I go into a grocer's store here and I'm loud or I laugh at something, everybody stares. On the tubes nobody speaks much or smiles. In New York they assault you with noise."

"I love being on stage and I love the expressions in people's eyes and the ecstasy and the thrill but I have to have a bodyguard now for security reasons. I feel caged in hotel rooms wherever I go. In New Orleans once I took a cab to Bourbon Street. I put on a hat and pulled it down low but as soon as I stepped on to the curb someone said 'There's Madonna'. It hasn't quite got to the point where I never go out yet. I still go running or shopping. I don't sit around contemplating my fame or how popular I am. What interests me is my confrontations with people every day and my performances at night. I don't sit and think about my record sales or how much money I have."

"People say I've set back the women's movement 30 years but I think that women weren't ashamed of their bodies in the 1950s. They luxuriated in their femininity and believed wholeheartedly in it. Women aren't like men. They can do things that men can't, mentally and physically. If people don't get the humour in my act, then they don't *want* to get it."

"I loved nuns when I was growing up. I thought they were beautiful. For several years I wanted to be a nun. I saw them as really pure, disciplined, above average people. They had these serene faces. Nuns are sexy. I also loved Carole Lombard, Judy Holliday, Marilyn Monroe. They were all incredibly funny, and they were silly and sweet. I just saw myself in them, my funniness, and my need to boss people around and at the same time be taken care of. My knowingness and my innocence. Both."

Discography

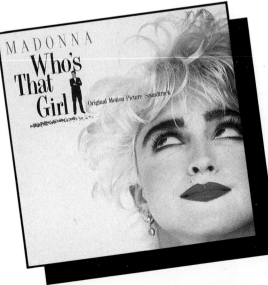